EXTREME SPORTS
An Imagination Library Series

TRIATHLONS

by John E. Schindler

Gareth Stevens
Publishing

Please visit our web site at: www.garethstevens.com
For a free color catalog describing Gareth Stevens Publishing's
list of high-quality books and multimedia programs,
call 1-800-542-2595 (USA) or 1-800-387-3178 (Canada).
Gareth Stevens Publishing's fax: (877) 542-2596

Library of Congress Cataloging-in-Publication Data

Schindler. John E.
    Triathlons / by John E. Schindler.
       p. cm. — (Extreme sports: an imagination library series)
    Includes bibliographical references and index.
    ISBN-10: 0-8368-4544-7 ISBN-13: 978-0-8368-4544-0 (lib. bdg.)
    ISBN-10: 0-8368-4551-X ISBN-13: 978-0-8368-4551-8 (softcover)
    1. Triathlon—Juvenile literature. 2. Triathlon—Training—Juvenile literature.
  I. Title. II. Extreme sports (Milwaukee, Wis.)
  GV1060.73.S35 2005
  796.42'57—dc22   2004062578

First published in 2005 by
Gareth Stevens Publishing
A Weekly Reader Company
1 Reader's Digest Rd.
Pleasantville, NY 10570-7000 USA

Text: John E. Schindler
Cover design and page layout: Tammy West
Series editor: Carol Ryback
Photo research: Diane Laska-Swanke

Photo credits: Cover, p. 17 © Clayton Chase/WireImage.com; pp. 5, 11, 13 © Martina
Sandkühler/Jump; p. 7 © Kristiane Vey/Jump; pp. 9, 19 © Action Images/WireImage.com;
p. 15 © Celeste Fowler/SeaPics.com; p. 21 © Chris Ivin/WireImage.com

Printed in the United States of America

3 4 5 6 7 8 9 10 09 08 07

Cover: Jenny Tobin, of Boise, Idaho,
becomes the first woman across the finish
line of Utah's first Ironman in 2002.

TABLE OF CONTENTS

Words that appear in the glossary are printed in **boldface** type the first time they occur in the text.

THREE IN ONE

Athletes like to enter races to test their skills. For most races, athletes do only one sport. They race to see who is the fastest swimmer, **cyclist**, or runner. A race that includes three sports is called a **triathlon**.

Each part of a triathlon is a different length. For most triathlons, the swimming part is about 1 mile (1.5 kilometers) long. The cycling part is about 25 miles (40 km) long. The running part is a little more than 6 miles (10 km) long.

Triathletes must not go too fast or too slow when swimming, cycling, or running. Their energy must last a long time.

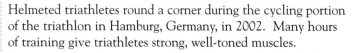

Helmeted triathletes round a corner during the cycling portion of the triathlon in Hamburg, Germany, in 2002. Many hours of training give triathletes strong, well-toned muscles.

ATHLETES OF IRON

The first **competitive** triathlon was held in San Diego, California, in 1974. Triathletes swam about 1 mile (1.5 km). They cycled 25 miles (40 km). They ran about 6 miles (10 km).

Some triathlons are much shorter. **Sprint**, or mini-, triathlons are very popular. A kids' triathlon might have a 200-yard (183-meter) swim, a 6-mile (10-km) bike ride, and a 1-mile (1.5-km) run.

Only the best triathletes in the world compete in the **Ironman** triathlon in Hawaii. They swim 2.4 miles (4 km), cycle 112 miles (180 km), and run 26 miles (42 km). "Extreme Iron" triathlons are even longer than the Ironman distances!

A wave of swimmers thrashes through the surf during the Ironman triathlon in Hawaii. **Rescue divers** on boats carry safety gear and offer help to swimmers when needed.

ON THE TRAINING TRACK

Triathlons can be fun, but they are hard to do.

You must train for hours every day. One day, you can swim. The next day, you might run. The third day, you can bike. After many months, you might do all three in one day.

You can also do **cross-training** workouts in a gym. Cross-training workouts help your whole body. Weight machines help you get stronger. Working out on a stair-stepper machine or a **treadmill** helps you keep moving for a long time.

You must also eat a healthy diet. Eat lots of fruit and vegetables. Drink at least eight glasses of water every day. Get enough sleep, too.

Triathlete Kate Allen of Austria (center) runs from the water after finishing the swimming part at the 2004 Olympics in Athens, Greece.

GO SOAK YOUR HEAD

Swimming is always the first part of a triathlon. It is one of the hardest exercises you can do. Even the best swimmers use a lot of energy.

You might wear a swim cap or goggles during the swimming race. In cold water, you might also wear a **wet suit**. A wet suit traps a layer of water inside your suit next to your skin. The water warms up as you swim to keep you warm.

Swimming becomes very dangerous when you are tired. Rescue divers watch the swimming race. They are ready to help you or other swimmers who may become too tired.

Goggles help swimmers see where they are going. Many triathlons require that both men and women wear numbered swim caps.

TIME FOR A CHANGE

After the swimming part of the triathlon, you jump on your bike. Changing from swimming to cycling is called a **transition**. You must put on your helmet and biking shoes during the transition.

Your transition should be as short as possible. A clock records how long you take in every part of the triathlon. It also records your transition time. Get on your bike quickly!

Are you still wet from the swim? Do not worry. The wind will dry you off during the bike race.

Now start pedaling!

Triathletes rush from the water for their transition to the cycling part of the triathlon. Some swimmers wear wet suits to protect against the cold water temperature.

ROLL ON DOWN THE ROAD

The cycling part of a triathlon happens on regular roads. You ride a racing bike. It should have very thin tires and weigh very little.

You should wear biking shoes that lock onto special bike pedals. The shoes and pedals let you push down and pull up on the pedals. Your muscles are always working during the cycling race.

The best way to ride a bike fast is with your arms stretched forward and your back flat. That position helps you move through the wind faster. Your helmet also helps cut through the wind.

Police often watch the roads during a triathlon to help keep cyclists safe.

The background becomes a colorful blur as a triathlete races down a road while training for the Hawaii Ironman. His body position helps him go faster.

RUN TO THE FINISH

You have one more race after the bike race. It is also time for another transition. Take off your helmet. Kick off your biking shoes. Put on your running shoes.

Your training will help you finish the running race. You may be very tired. Keep going. You trained for this!

You will see many people helping during each part of the triathlon. They are called **volunteers** because they do not get paid for their work. Volunteers help the triathlon go smoothly. They might hand out water. They might direct traffic. Some volunteers help with first aid in case someone gets hurt.

A volunteer grabs the bike as Teri Duthie of Boulder, Colorado, transitions to the running part of Utah's first-ever Ironman in 2002. She must quickly take off her helmet and put on running shoes for the last part of the triathlon.

SEE YOU NEXT YEAR?

A triathlon might be named after a person. Another triathlon could be named for where it takes place. A triathlon could also be named for a company. Some triathlons are held at the same time and place every year.

Some athletes only want to do a triathlon once in their lives. Other athletes like to enter two or more triathlons every year. Athletes who enter a lot of triathlons are always training.

Most of the people who compete in triathlons do it just to see if they can finish. They want to test their bodies and stay healthy.

Olympic triathletes race along a palm-tree-lined street in Athens, Greece, in 2004.

WORKING BODIES HARD

You did it! You crossed the finish line! Your body worked hard, and you feel tired, but in a good way.

If you win a triathlon, you might get a medal or a big prize. You might even become famous!

Chances are you will look for another triathlon to enter. You will try to finish in a shorter time. You might also try doing a triathlon in a different part of the country. You could do a few sprint triathlons to help you stay in shape.

You can keep training for triathlons your whole life. You might say you are hooked on triathlons!

Canadian Lisa Bentley focuses on finishing the cycling part of the Australian Ironman Triathlon in April, 2004. She took first place overall.

MORE TO READ AND VIEW

Books (Nonfiction)   *Running. Working Out* (series). Jeff Savage.
(Crestwood House)

Swimming. Successful Sports (series). John Verrier.
(Heinemann)

Triathlon. Extreme Sports (series). Bill Lund.
(Capstone)

Triathlons for Kids. Sally Edwards.
(Winning International)

Books (Fiction)   *Get Set! Swim!* Jeannine Atkins.
(Lee & Low Books)

Pushing the Limits. Generation Girl, No. 3 (series).
Melanie Stewart. (Golden Books)

DVDs and Videos   *Triathlon: Training and Racing.* (Delta Library)

Quest for the Gold – Triathlon.
Sydney 2000 Olympics. (NBC Film Clips)

WEB SITES

Web sites change frequently, but the following web sites should last awhile. You can also search Google (*www.google.com*) or Yahooligans! (*www.yahooligans.com*) for more information about triathlons. Some keywords to help your search include: *kids triathlons, competitive swimming, cycling for kids, Ironman, junior racing, Olympic triathlons, training for kids.*

www.bratclub.com.au/
Discover triathlons for kids "Down Under" in Australia. Follow the careers of some of these future world-class athletes.

www.kidsofsteel.com
Watch a short video clip of "Toe Belly Up Belly," a workout video that takes kids from warm-up to cool-down.

www.kidsrunning.com/krask.html
Visit this Runner's World microsite to find links to training, cross-training, stretching exercises, and health and nutrition tips.

www.triathlon.org
Find out about triathlons all over the world.

GLOSSARY

You can find these words on the pages listed. Reading a word in a sentence helps you understand it even better.

athletes — people who like to do sports. 4, 18

competitive — having a goal of winning. 6

cross-training — doing more than one type of exercise to get stronger. 8

cyclist — a person who rides a bike. 4, 14

Ironman — a triathlon with very long distances for each part. 6, 14, 16, 20

rescue divers — safety divers who are ready to offer help to swimmers. 6, 10

sprint — doing something for a short distance in a burst of high speed. 6, 20

transition — a change. 12, 16

treadmill — a workout machine that lets you walk or run at different speeds and at many angles for a set amount of time. 8

triathletes — athletes who compete in triathlons. 4, 6, 8, 14, 18

triathlon — a race with three parts. 4, 6, 8, 10, 12, 14, 16, 18, 20

volunteers — people who help because they want to, not for money. 16

wet suit — a rubber suit worn in cold water that helps keep a swimmer warm. 10

INDEX